Feminist Werewolf

Katie Anthony

For my girls
and my boys

CONTENTS

Wake up every morning
and tell yourself
that you're a badass bitch from hell
and that no one can fuck with you
and then don't let anybody fuck with you.

Kate Nash

I have a feminist werewolf.
She comes out way more often than the full moon.
She eats the men who try to explain her to me.
She is sharp and filthy and focused.
I love her.

Katie Anthony

Dinosaur Defense

My son explains
that stegosaurus had spiky plates on its back
to protect it from predators
who wanted to eat it all up.

I say, "Baby
you're growing inside and out."

When boys grow inside and out
you hope you've raised them gently;
when girls grow inside and out
you hope you've raised them strong.

Girls grow up inside;
they grow up out;
and before you know it
"honey"
starts to sound
different
when it drips
from the lips
of men with sweet teeth.

You need to know 3 things
before I go any further:

1. I was not beautiful
the first time a grown man
blew me a slow kiss.
I was bespectacled
and slouching,
selecting a steno pad at a gas station
and seven years old.

2. I was not beautiful
the first time a classmate
passed me in the hall
and hollered
nice whoppers
as his friends fist-pumped and cheered.

I was bespectacled
and slouching,
a hardback, plastic-wrapped
Stephen King book from the library
pressed against my aching chest.
I was thirteen.

3. I was beautiful
on my wedding day.
And nobody said or did a goddamned thing
to remind me that I
was about to get fucked.

If it were a compliment
men wouldn't say it
only when we're alone.

If it's a compliment
why does it feel
like they're sounding me,
dragging across the stone of my face
to see if I crumble
or crush.

If it were a compliment
I would not have to take out my headphones
and check over my shoulder
at the approach of every jogger
until I shoot the deadbolt home.

Cut the shit,
animal of a man.
It's not a compliment.

His voice, his face
his body rising from the bench as I walk by,
they are all reminders
that if I pass whole
it is because
he allowed it.

He stood up as I approached and nodded,
framing me in his hands like a subject.
"Oh honey,
you got a sexy ass body baby.
I know you can hear me.
Hey.
Hey.
HEY.
Smile, bitch."

Two passed me on the well-lit street
where I chose to walk

when the light got low
and they reached a consensus
out loud
as they turned around
to follow me back they way they'd come.

"Mmmmmmmm,
nice,"
said the first.
"Beautiful woman,"
said the second.

I was not beautiful.
I was alone.

Being the mother of sons has given me
the perfect explanation
for the tingling in a woman's back
when she knows the man behind her
is not going anywhere
except where she goes.

We want armor to puncture our skin.
We, the smaller, slower species,
wish for bodies
that could shatter the jaws of predators.

I was not beautiful.
I was alone.

After they turned back
with a final blown kiss,
I let my mind rehearse
what I'd do when they came back,
that house has its lights on.

I let my mind wonder:
What did I do wrong?

I could have stopped walking.

I wish I'd turned
and screwed a stare into them
until they grew uncomfortable
(but then what)
(then you've dared them).

Even silence is dangerous.

I wish I'd turned.
I wish I'd charged them
and howled
and pounded my chest
and spat
and thrown garbage at them
and scratched the pavement
and bared my teeth
and growled
"My skin is plated armor
and I'll break your jaws,
you try to eat me up
motherfucker."

I wish I'd gone crazy
enough to pit their stomachs.

I wish the sight of my face
peeled open
would follow them home
so they'd hurry along
checking over their shoulder
at the sound of every jogger.

I wish all of us would do this.

I wish men would get nervous
when they see our smaller bodies walking
closer
and closer.
Is this one okay?
or is this one
a stegosaurus too?

I wish they'd be embarrassed.
I wish every time they worried,
they remembered every time before
and felt lucky to have gotten away
so many times.

Maybe then they'd understand
our accumulated, defensive dread,
the way we must mistrust an entire species
to survive.
Our blood taught us that much.

I wish women would murmur under their breaths
at men who sit on benches alone at dusk:

"Oh honey
you got a hungry look in your eye.
But I have 17 plates
sewn into the skin of my spine
and they are there to make you bleed
if you try to take a bite out of me
bitch."

The Fox in the Hen House

I thought I was doing everything right.

Our library is stocked with kickass woman picture books about Amelia Earhart, Malala, Lucille Ball, Rosie Revere, and the Paper Bag Princess. I never force my children to hug or kiss anyone.

I encourage my sons to explore lots of toys, clothes, and interests, not just "boy" things. Buster is 3, and his favorite outfit is a jazzy little workout set in pink and turquoise. Chicken, 5, gets regular mani-pedis in our home "salon," complete with cucumber water in a sippy cup.

My husband and I consciously subvert traditional gender roles; he cooks, cleans, kisses boo-boos, and yearns for a room of his own. I sit in an armchair by the fire with a scotch and the evening paper and bark at the children to "Pipe down, ya mongrels." Because feminism.

I educate myself about how to limit their exposure to dudebro dirtbaggery and magnify feminist heroism. Sexist soccer coaches, gendered Legos, parents of other kids who tell their sons that "big boys don't cry," I was ready to take on all of the BS.

I had great ideas about how to protect my kids against the damage that the world will try to do to them. But what I didn't remember, what was far harder and far more painful to consider, was how to protect my kids against the damage that the world has already done to me.

———

I reminded Buster to grab his water bottle. He shook his head, sighed, and muttered, "so stupid," on his way back to the counter. I didn't have to ask where he heard that kind of talk. I said it. I say it almost every day. Not about him, of course. About myself.

When I finally get all the kids and backpacks and rain boots out the door to the car, and I reach into my pocket for the keys and realize I left them on the counter… (sigh) *so stupid.*

When I leave my sunglasses on the roof of the car. *Nice one, dummy.* When I lose my shit and scream at the kids about which color cheese sticks I packed in their lunch. *Ugh, I'm crazy.*

When I decide to read a book or watch TV instead of matching the kids' socks and the next day I have to spelunk in the sock hamper for mismatched socks (again). *I was lazy last night.*

I hear moms everywhere I go using words like this – dumb, silly, crazy, stupid – not about their children (we would never say things like that to our children!) but about themselves. The problem is that the words we use around our children become their words, too. The way we talk to them, and to ourselves, is the way they will talk to others. And themselves.

———

I've been a parent for about 5 years. I've been a girl for 32. I am a feminist, but I was born and raised behind enemy lines. My underlying chromosomal

8

makeup can't compete with 32 years of hardcore, unrelenting conditioning that has taught me that my chromosomal makeup and its physical expression is at best second-class, inconsequential, and strange, and at worst a weapon, a weakness, a tawdry distraction to these good men just trying to do the Lord's work over here.

Equality, respect, and safety for women are in my best interests, yet STILL I catch myself disliking "abrasive" or "chilly" female CEOs for reasons that I don't stop to question, and swooning whenever a famous man recites the line fed to him by his publicist, that "women are people too."

#OhMyGodHesSoNice
#HeThinksImAPerson
#WhatACatch
#ThatIsHumiliating
#LetsRaiseTheBarPeople

My conscious mind wants to smash the patriarchy; my unconscious habits snuggle comfortably at his slippered feet.

The day I heard my not-yet-3-year-old call himself stupid, something he learned by listening to me, was the day I started to notice how much I talk shit about myself. That was the day I realized there was a fox in my hen house.

———

Meet The Fox. He's been in my head for as long as I can remember.

He told me that I should wear flimsy slick-bottomed ballet flats that looked like Cinderella's, that made me slip on the hillside when I chased after the boys in their rugged-soled boots. He crooned, "See? Wasn't that easier?" when I smiled prettily and agreed with the loudest voice in the room.

He told me I was fat when I was 11. He shook his head when I lost my temper and everyone said I was crazy or bleeding from wherever.

I live every minute of every day with a fat-mouth, fat-head, bag-a-dicks fox in my hen house, and he never stops telling me that I'm not good enough, and I've spent most of my life agreeing with him because he is the loudest voice in that room.

When I veto the Batman DVD for movie night because it's too violent: *You are such a silly little girl.*

When I remember to call the cable company: *Wow, slow clap for you. It took you a week and a half to make one phone call. Are you even an adult? Would you even have a functioning life if you didn't have a husband to take care of the REAL stuff?*

When I'm white-knuckling the steering wheel as I attempt to negotiate peace between one kid who wants to listen to Disney Storybook Favorites and the other kid who wants Frog and Toad: *Get a grip, crazy lady. It's not like you're curing cancer here.*

If The Fox had a central thesis, it would look something like this:

It is important for you to understand that no matter what you do or how hard you work, you can never take pride in your accomplishments or feel valuable or competent.

I will take every opportunity to remind you that your work doesn't matter; that your mistakes are proof that you will never be a worthwhile person; that your thoughts, opinions, and feelings are less important than mine and based in silly irrational nonsense; that you do not deserve to have time, space, or a voice; and that your only value lies in the pleasant feelings you can give me by being nice and pretty, and the work you can do to support me.

———

There's a fine line we have to be aware of – the line between inviting women to recognize that they deserve good treatment, and blaming women for their own poor treatment. I am doing the first one. Not the second one.

I am saying that when I called myself stupid, lazy, or worthless, I was talking to myself in a voice that was not my own. I'm not telling you how to be or how to talk. You are already great.

I am telling The Fox, the one who calls you a stupid, lazy, dumb, crazy, inconsequential, worthless, silly, hot mess, train wreck, boring, pathetic loser, to sit down and shut up.

We are reclaiming our time.

———

I began to practice positive self-talk in front of my kids.

You might hear me walking the canned bean aisle at the grocery store, declaring in the voice of the Yia-Yia Sisterhood, "I MAKE THOUGHTFUL CHOICES ABOUT NUTRITION BECAUSE I AM SMART AND STRONG. THIS WEEK, WE BUY KIDNEY BEANS."

You might see me screech to a stop in the parking lot, get out of the car, and pull down my iced coffee from where I left it on the roof, and pronounce in a voice stentorian with years of theatre training, "I REMEMBERED MY ICED COFFEE. I REMEMBER MANY IMPORTANT THINGS."

I have begun to say good things about myself, loudly and often. It is uncomfortable and people probably think I am bizarrely confident. But I am doing it anyway.

Because before I do anything else to raise my kids to be feminists, I have to identify and address the way The Fox demands that I try to reach unreachable standards for women's beauty, silence, and virtue, and then makes me feel shitty for falling short, being too loud or messy or ambitious or mean, demanding more space, wearing clunky sneakers, or chewing my hair.*

I have to see how the world has damaged me first. Because I don't hear women say good things about themselves very much. Because a child could take that to mean that women can't think of anything good to say about themselves. Because the voice we use to talk to our kids (and to ourselves) will become the voice in their heads.

Because I wouldn't let a sexist soccer coach talk like that to my kids. I wouldn't let a teacher, babysitter, uncle, or friend talk like that to my kids. Because I won't let my sons learn how to talk to themselves, or to any person, like a Fox.

———

The Fox tells you that you can't do anything right. Let me flip a switch for you.

Every day you pick up 400 objects from where you left them the night before, and you start to juggle them again. All of the objects are different sizes, shapes, weights. They all require your constant touch to keep them in motion. They all require a different touch.

You juggle a feather, a soup pot, and a belt.

You juggle nutrition, empathy, and trash day.

You juggle a single piece of paper that you need to sign and return today, that flutters and swoops unpredictably, that falls to the ground.

The Fox says, "You are so stupid."

I say, "Look at you. You are a marvel, an athlete, an X-woman. Look at the way you keep the world spinning for your family. Look at the way you can pick that up again. It shouldn't be possible for a person to do all that at the same time, but you do it, and you make it look easy. You are amazing."

You are amazing. Tell your kids. Tell yourself. You are amazing.

Chewing my hair WAS super gross. I can't even defend it by saying I was trying to subvert misogynistic standards of female beauty. I can still remember the way single strands of hair would get stuck between my teeth as I bit the clump of hair flat, gnawing on it as happily and absently as a puppy on a rope knot.

I had a single damp, shiny dreadlock that smelled like Johnson's baby shampoo and morning breath. It hung next to my right ear until my mother cut my hair so short I couldn't chew it anymore. I mean. The Fox had a point there.

Girl Blank Face

If you've never seen an episode of Lie To Me or taken a Cosmo Body Language Quiz, then you probably wouldn't have given the couple at the bar a second glance.

But I have seen every episode of Lie to Me because Tim Roth, and I have taken at least 700 Body Language Quizzes, so I could see shit was going down.

They sat on two bar stools at a slick little modern Italian bistro. Both in their late 20's or early 30's, both drinking red wine.

He was probably 5'10", fit and boxy, dressed neatly like a prep school wrestler. He wore a pink polo and dark brown khakis, and the ribbed cuff of his short sleeves cut into the slabs of his arms. He sat sideways in his bar stool, leaning forward, his whole body pointed at her. His legs spread open (easy there, chief), his right foot rested on the crossbar of her stool (we get it), and his right hand gripped her seat back (are you going to pee on her now?). He kept gesturing broadly with his left hand, craning his neck around to try to meet her eyes, and occasionally his right index finger would pop up to stroke her back.

She was probably 5'8", average build, with a thick riot of blonde curls. She was dressed like she'd come from work at a law office. Her cobalt blue cardigan covered slender arms; the conservative black pencil skirt hem rested at her kneecaps while she was sitting, which meant it fell to the top of her calves when she stood. She sat stiffly with her legs crossed away from him (hello) and leaning back (red flag) with her shoulders angled toward the bar (help her immediately) and her left arm casually wrapped around her stomach (she might as well be macing him).

Every time he made a joke (I could tell because he'd laugh, and lay his left hand on her drink hand) she leveled him with an expression so flat, cool, and impassive that it honestly would have hurt him less to get hit in the face with a frisbee made of gravel and ice.

It's called Girl Blank Face. I know it well, and you probably do, too. GBF is an expression that some might categorize as "bored," or "vacant," or "drunk." And they're right! This is a totally normal facial expression for a person to have in the following scenarios:

1. Waiting in line at the DMV
2. Stuck in traffic with a broken car radio and a dead cell phone with nothing to do but think about your life choices
3. Six chardonnays deep, watching 27 Dresses

Make no mistake. The difference between Regular Blank Face and Girl Blank Face has nothing to do with the expression itself, and everything to do with the *context* in which the Face is served. In the context of a boring fucking afternoon at the post office, ain't no thang. In other contexts... well...

1. "Smile honey. Look, you're so pretty now!"

2. "Yes, you were obviously qualified for this position. But we felt that Rick was a better fit. Besides, this way you can still have life balance. How's that baby, by the way?"
3. (A man is staring at you from across the aisle on the bus. He gets up and takes the seat next to you.)

Girl Blank Face is an evolutionary tool, a mask we pull down when we feel under siege, a way of hiding and defusing and keeping everything even and fine, just fine. I think it's a learned survival mechanism, something girls learn when the first girl in the middle school starts wearing a bra, and the boy who stands behind her in chorus snaps it during the Christmas concert and even the chorus teacher laughs a little.

When I was a girl I hit a boy for calling me Whoppers and I got sent to the office, Girl Blank Face firmly set as I was offered my choice of baggy KMart sweaters from the Dress Code Violation Bin.

Sure, in a perfect world he would have apologized to me and I wouldn't have had to spend the rest of the day among my giggling classmates with my girl body sheathed in a XXL bright green and yellow striped polyester sweater that fell to my knees. But the world isn't going to be perfect, and at least I didn't cry in the lunchroom.

Girl Blank Face is a mask. It protects us from being labeled "weak" or "emotional" or "bitchy" or "shrill." Girl Blank Face is a shield. It protects us from looking afraid, or angry, or humiliated, or intense. Girl Blank Face is, like all masks and shields, both a comfort and a shame.

This is the face you see on a woman who is being hit on while locked in a steel box with a stranger who looks at her body and makes her legs tingle: *Run.* She's watching the numbers light up, one by one, as the elevator climbs to her floor. *Run.*

This is the face you see on a woman who has just been complimented, out loud, in the break room, on the fit of her jeans. *Just pretend you didn't hear it.*

This is the face I made when a distant relation told me to watch Super Nanny so I could be a better parent. *That really hurts my feelings and also fuck you.*

This face means:

1. Okay. Just get it out of your system so I can leave.
2. Don't cry. Don't cry. Don't cry.
3. You scare me.
4. You are a piece of shit and you scare me.
5. Don't touch me.
6. I don't want to talk to you.
7. Get me out of here.

That last one was probably what the girl at the bar was thinking. The guy wasn't holding her at knifepoint or anything, at least not explicitly, at least not knowingly, but when a man that size is that close, he doesn't need another weapon to become a threat.

The guy went to the bathroom, trailing his hand across her back as he passed her stool. As soon as he rounded the corner, she pulled a $20 out of where she'd tucked it in her skirt waistband, presumably after she'd gone to the bathroom and found no back door out of this joint. She slapped the bill on the bar, waved to the bartender, pointed to the money, and dashed into the street. She didn't stop to look around but if she had, she would have seen every woman there giving her the Hunger Games salute.

When the guy returned, found her gone, and scanned the room with a furrowed brow for a flash of cobalt blue, he saw a whole sea of Girl Blank Faces. I can only assume he was confused for a moment. We must have all looked so familiar. I imagine he was thinking, "Do i know her? She looks so familiar. I feel like i've seen that face somewhere before. Oh! You know what it is. That blank stare. It's 100% Trish. You know, Trish from work? She wore those white jeans one time? Her. Yeah. I almost got her number one time on the elevator, but she got off before I could. She must've been late or something. That was before she had the baby. Yeah, did you hear? Rick got that promotion! I know, good for him. But yeah, anyway. That face. Classic Trish."

Have You Ever

Let me just ask you this.

Have you ever been touched
without your permission?

By your arm?
By a friendly grandpa type?
By your back?
By a Greenpeace volunteer?
(They don't touch everyone, you know.
They don't touch my husband.)

Have you ever looked
across a coffee shop
and met the eyes
of a panting man
watching you?

Have you ever had to weigh
that if you turned and walked away
he'd keep going,
anyway?

Have you ever stood your ground
because *fuck you*

because
look at my face?
Because you wanted to be able
to see him?

Have you ever wished for a coat?

Have you ever hated yourself
for the clothes you chose?
Have you ever thought
what did you expect would happen?

Have you ever laughed,
and kissed a man's cheek
when he appeared out of nowhere
three blocks from home
and said
"Let me walk you,
you're beautiful,
let me walk you.
Are you close?
I'll walk you.
What's your name."

Have you ever laughed and refused,
laughed and refused,
laughed as he walked with you anyway
laughed as you thought
where can I go
laughed until you let him spank you,
lightly,
good-bye?

Have you ever been saved
by your willingness
to bend over?

Have you ever realized
how often laughing works?

Have you ever laughed
and understood immediately
that this one does not like
to be laughed at?

Have you ever been saved?

Have you ever had to thank a stranger
for pulling you away
from a stranger
when he saw your blank face
the picture of animal panic
when your back was on the wall?

Have you ever hated the man who helped you
because it was just
just
just
humiliating
that you had a hero?
To thank?
For what?
Nothing happened.
You just
got pushed into a wall
for a minute
or two.

Have you ever
hugged someone tight
like a boxer does?
Have you ever pressed yourself against

the person who wants
to take you?
Have you ever waited out the clock?

Have you ever been saved
when a stranger realized
that someone else already had dibs
on you?

Have you ever heard
one man
apologize
to another
for nearly taking you?

Because he didn't realize
you
were
his?

Sorry, man.
I didn't know
she was yours.

Have you ever tried to speak
after being saved
like that?

Have you ever found your jaw
tight as a tomb
after being saved
like that?

Have you ever seen them perfect their signals
like a pitcher and a catcher?
Have you ever seen them lob the ball

with underhanded grace?

Have you ever been
the ball?

"Aren't you happy to see my friend?
Don't you want to say hello?
Show him how you say hello.
She's the best."

Have you ever had the sense
that there was already a plan
for your evening?

And that it would be best
to get okay with it?

Have you ever caught a glimpse of a wink
a nod
over your head
when you smiled
and hugged the man
you were supposed to hug?

When he hugged you high
and low
testing all the edges of your soft,
round parts
just to see
if you had
a line?

Have you ever played along?

Have you ever smiled
at someone who scares you?

Have you ever
gone quiet
and chosen to permit
what was going to happen?

Have you ever pretended
you love to give blow jobs
because you wanted to leave
unfucked?

Have you ever let your boyfriend
take pictures of you
and found out
years later
that everyone
(everyone)
saw them?

Have you ever been surprised
like that?
Years later,
engaged,
catching up
with an old friend?

Have you ever been
so unsurprised?

Have you ever thought
well what did you think would happen?

Have you ever gone blank?
Have you ever thrown little pebbles
at the advancing tank?

Wait
Wait
Wait wait wait wait wait
WAIT

Have you ever been told
to consent?

Have you ever gone toe-to-toe
on a summer afternoon
at a cafe table full of crosstalking smart young people
like you,
people you've just met and like,
making some pretty good points
actually,
making everyone laugh
until the man you were arguing with
told you to shut up and put your tits away?

Have you ever shut up
and covered
what wasn't uncovered?
Have you ever taken a slap
like that?
Quietly?

Have you ever been saved
from that silent table?

Have you ever had to thank
the person who saved you?

Have you ever said thank you?

Or do you just
get

too
mad?

No Eggs, No Basket

I wouldn't say I've spent the last 3 years on any kind of "scene," unless you call a working knowledge of the PBS Kids universe a "scene." If so, then I am a Dinosaur Train club rat. Daniel Tiger is my jam!

I can count on two hands the number of times I've worn high heels in the last three years, and not one of those occasions was one in which I would have called myself "tarted up." No, I didn't rock a leather minidress and gallons of eyeliner at the casual Christmas party, or on a date night to see Anthony Bourdain, or a trip to the opera with a close girlfriend.

Don't worry - I don't feel sorry for myself. I'm used to my invisibility now. I'm even comforted by my superficial sexlessness when I buy a pack of sliced mangoes at Trader Joe's, two little boys in tow. Ain't nobody grinding up on me at Day Out with Thomas the Train. I do not worry about the heavy-lidded barista slipping something in my Americano at Starbucks.

You're talking to a girl who had to start wearing a bra at 11. I tried to close my shoulders like a bird in a storm when the gray-stubbled long-haul trucker at the gas station licked his lips and blew me a kiss, the summer before 8th grade.

Sure, sometimes I miss the validation of an automatic over-the-shoulder butt-check when I walk by.

But for the most part I'm relieved not to be a hot piece. In fact, I just got back from a weekend in Vegas where I was relieved when the roving bands of greased-up, Axe-sprayed, boner-tucked dudes paid me no mind.

My maxi dresses and wedding ring might as well have been a Maryknoll Nun's habit and crucifix. It was so great to be left alone. Except sometimes when it wasn't.

For most of my life, I kept all of my eggs in a "pretty" basket, because I got a shitload of feedback on how important it was to be pretty. The first word to describe every Disney princess? Fair. Lovely. Beautiful.

I will never forget the time when, in the middle of an eye-stabbingly dull conversation, a frat guy said, "It's a good thing you're hot, because otherwise nobody would ever want to talk to you. You're not really, you know, fun or interesting."

I said, "Wow" and walked away as I bit my cheek and wished I were the kind of person who would say, "Maybe you're the boring one, you dick," or throw a drink in his face. I felt so sad, but not because he'd called me boring. I was sad because I secretly agreed with him. Exhibit A: he brutally cut me halfway down to the ground, and I voluntarily shrunk the rest of the way. I wasn't that smart compared to a lot of smart people. I wasn't that funny compared to a lot of funny people. But I could hike my boobs up and make new friends all night long.

But at some point, when I moved to New York and became an actress, I had to accept that I was, if not an ugly duckling, perhaps a three-beers-pretty chipmunk.

I began to move all of my eggs, every single one, from the pretty basket to the interesting basket. I don't regret that move. I chose to let the pretty basket head on downstream. There is no universe in which I'd rather be dumb and cute.

But a funny thing happened when I stopped gauging my worth by my appearance... I started to think my appearance was worthless.

I should have been thinking, "It doesn't matter if I look good, because I am a good and interesting person." But instead I've been thinking, "Good thing I'm an interesting person, because I do not look good."

Sometime in the days since I decided that there were more important things than turning heads, I started to believe that I *have* to be interesting, because pretty is no longer an option. That frat guy is still in my head, only this time he's saying, "It's a good thing you're funny and interesting because nobody would want to talk to you otherwise. You're not really, like, hot." God, I wish I knew his name. I would totally find him on Facebook and sign him up for taxidermy catalogues and erectile dysfunction newsletters.

There comes a time in every woman's life, or at least the time has come in this woman's life, when she looks in the mirror and says, "Well shit. I have to start drinking more water." As if dehydration were the culprit, rather than time, just time, just days and years pulling bits of beauty down to the ground to lie like dust in our footprints.

The thing is, it's those days and years that make us so much fucking better than we were - funny, smart, strong, irreverent, bold, and yes, last and least, a little sad when we catch the first glimpse of the empty skin that hangs from our upper arms.

And if my days and years have helped me to become anything, it's more aware of the inconsistency of identity and personality. Now more than ever I know how dangerous it is to try to cram your whole personality into one trait, to place all your eggs in one basket. Imagine if Michael Jordan felt that he were only a person of worth so long as he was the best basketball player in the world. I'll tell you one thing, the world would be a little bit sadder without those Hanes Tagless Tee commercials.

It was funny being in Las Vegas. Even though I'm old enough to know better, the impulse to impress strangers lives deep and hard, a tulip bulb defying the frost to emerge through the cracked Earth at the first hint of sun. All it took was one bachelor party in suits and white smiles, and I sat up like a well-trained cocker spaniel. *Hey! Here! Me! I'm still pretty! Right? Guys? Guys?*

Walking through the casino at midnight on Saturday I felt a little schizophrenic. Simultaneous, contradictory thoughts wove a broken pattern in my head:

> *Those guys are so cute.*
> *I wonder if they think I'm cute.*
> *It doesn't matter if they think I'm cute.*
> *I'm not cute anymore. And that's okay.*
> *And I'm really sad.*
> *Is it over?*
> *It's not over.*
> *You should smile at them.*
> *Don't smile at them.*
> *You should see if you can get one of them to buy you a drink.*
> *Girl, this is Vegas. Ain't no cute guy dropping $26 on a cocktail for a married mother of two.*
> *God, I don't miss this.*
> *God, I miss this.*
> *Those girls look skanky.*
> *Thank God I don't look skanky.*
> *I wish I looked a little skanky.*

I still care about how I look. I care enough, at least, to put on a hat if Chicken looks at me and says, "You've got that scary hair, Mommy." I care enough to make sure that my shoes match and that my shirt mostly fits. Some people might call those efforts habitual for a functioning adult, but the only habits I call my own these days are for caffeine and putting my hand over the pointy edge of the table when I can tell Buster is about to stand up.

So I can't say whether I try because I still yearn to be pretty, or I try because I have a scrap of self-respect left after the great Target-pants-wetting of aught-nine. Regardless, it takes effort to reach par on pretty these days, and I am simultaneously sad, and far too busy to wallow now that Buster has discovered that the "lock" on the snack cupboard is just a piece of painter's tape.

Thank God for my kids. Thanks to them I can adopt a preemptive nonchalance when it comes to opting out of the unofficial hot-or-not-off that is the life of a woman.

Listen, I'm not a 10. Obviously. But you should know that I'm aware of my rank. I have gracefully stepped aside, to allow cuter buns than mine to beautify the world and make your day. I have two kids and give no fucks.

Also I write a blog with, like, seriously 25 readers now. I have more important things to do than squats and my hair.

The best part? I believe me. I'm about ready to lose those eggs, and those baskets. I'm done being one thing. Nobody is just one thing, least of all me. It's a good thing I'm a *mom,* because...

Oh shit.

Great Moms

You are a great mom
is what I'm supposed to say.

I wrote it in a card today
and immediately frowned, angry
that I'd written in pen.

Whenever someone tells me
you're a great mom
my first thought is:
you have no idea;
the only thing you know about my parenting
is the parenting I have chosen to perform for you.

And my second thought is:
so you've been evaluating me?
So you've formed an opinion on the matter?

You're a great mom
feels like
we've all been observing your choices.
Yep, you've been scored
by everyone you trusted when you were low
and hey - good news!
We have decided

you pass.
Keep up the good work.

Pride demands
I toss my head
when it's patted like that.
Good girl.

Today, my dear friend,
my mother, my comrade,
the day we're supposed to get so many bouquets
and accolades, you need to hear me say:

you're not a great mom.

A great mom
is someone who aged out
of the braided hair of a good girl.

You are not a great mom.
You are not
domesticated.

You're not smooth,
simple,
or delighted by simplicity.

You are not a great mom.
Your benevolence is not bottomless.
You forget things.
Your temper is a force.
You're afraid.

You're not great
like
pleasant

like a great cookie recipe
that's been tuned to perfection.

You're not great
like
crafted
like a great novel
that's been edited
and scrapped
and pieced back together
within a pleasing cover.

You are great
like
vast
like the force of gravity,
like the universe
that we live in
but cannot know.

Like an army,
gut-trusting and sharp,
millions of eyes,
millions of arms.

You drop your compass.
You fall to the earth and scrabble,
dust in your eyes.
You growl "fuck!"

You are great
and terrible,
a tempest.

Tonight you pour a glass of water,
your first for the day.

The child reaches for it,
says please.

You give it.
The cup can be refilled.

Or.

You say *no*.
This is mine.
You drink while he cries.
The cup can be refilled.

You are great
like the tide.
You rear up,
you swell,
and all the shattered fragments
return to shore in your body.

You are the force
that moves the enormous cradle
where everything was born.

You are in pain.

When the baby cries
there's nothing to do but rise for him.
Because you are great
like the sun:
consuming yourself,
prehistoric,
imperative.

You are not a great mom.
You are not a great anything.

You are great.

You are great
and powerful.
You count to three.
Your fingers snap.
You hold a cloth
under the cold tap,
press it to his lip,
and watch the blood bloom.

You sit on the ground
any ground.
You rock him.
You press your lips to him.
You sing.
You are a fortress.

You, my friend.
I'm talking about you.

You are in the city,
a child on each hip,
and crowds part for you.
Your legs devour the ground
in long, strong strides.
Your children ride on you
as if you were their elephant.
You sweat.
You sing.

You see the backyard gate standing open.
You run.
The world better pray
your boys are okay

because you are great
and savage.

They wander in the empty street.
You scoop them up,
a child on each hip,
and you do not tear them to pieces
because you are great
and shaking.

Someone says
you are a great mom.

When I hear that I think
someone thinks we are a simple thing,
complete and content
within four walls.

You are great
like the world is great,
holding everything that has ever been born
in its body.

You are the heart.
Not the paper valentine.
The thundering drum.

When someone calls you
a great mom
know that what they mean is this:
you are great.

Consento

I don't want to.
You have to.
But I'm not ready.
It's time.
No.
No.
No.

In college theatre class, we did these acting exercises in pairs. The teacher gave us a short dialogue that could be imbued with any number of meanings. Like the one above, it could be between a mother and son, changing his diaper, or taking him to rehab. Between a doctor and a patient with a fear of needles, between a husband and wife in the delivery room.

No matter what setup you choose, though, I think it's clear that this is not a conversation between equals. At the end of the day, I think it's clear that one person has the power.

I think a lot about power in my days as a parent of two high-spirited boys. I yearn for power; I say "please bring back that open cup of chocolate pudding, it is 8:30

in the morning and food stays at the table," and my words seem to vanish like fruit flies after you pick up the apple.

Maybe "yearn" isn't the right word. I don't recline on a chaise while penning correspondence to my third cousin in Charleston about how deeply I *yearn* to be obeyed by my spirited offspring. There's nothing wistful about how badly I want to have an X-Man mutation for mind control.

Maybe I thirst for power. Maybe I lust. Oh, if I could just say "Stop!" and see his body freeze, locked, under my command... Instead, I say "Stop!" and he scampers away, and I have two new certainties to live with:

1. I just got owned by a three-year-old.

2. There is a new priority load of chocolate pudding-coated couch cushion covers that skips to the top of the priority list. Because there was definitely nothing else I needed to do with that time.

I've read all the books about teaching respect by modeling respect. I agree with them. I've seen how my son begins to flail when I take his hand, unbidden, unasked. The quickest way to freak him out is to attempt to hold him without first requesting access, and then quietly waiting to see if he grants it. He isn't a cuddler.

So I use words. A lot of words. If I do have to use my hand to redirect him, I announce it first, I say why, and I stop as soon as I can. *Chicken, I'm not going to let you throw that train. I'm taking the train so I can keep you and your brother safe. It is going on this shelf now. We will try again with the train later.*

Simple daily tasks require multiple and repeated reminders.

Chicken, in 5 minutes it's going to be time to use the potty.
    In 4 minutes, it's going to be time to use the potty.
    In 3 minutes, it's going to be time to use the potty.
    In 2 minutes, it's going to be time to use the potty.
    In 1 minute, it's going to be time to use the potty.
    There goes the timer! It's time to use the potty.

(He is surprised to hear this.)

I hear that you are not ready yet.
    You're upset because you don't want to stop playing to use the potty.
    It is time to use the potty.
    You can choose to walk to the potty, or I am going to help you put on a diaper, because if you're going to wear undies you have to use the potty.
    Thank you for coming to use the potty.
    Please take off your undies.
    No, baby, you have to take off your undies before you use the potty.

I hear that you want to use the potty with your undies on.

Yes, I know that bit was too long to be funny. Because, in life, it takes too long to be funny. Everything - *everything* - requires that level of intense engagement: putting on shoes, eating eggs, picking a story.

But the worst, hardest part is not how hard I have to fight him. The worst part is how hard I have to fight myself. Because I want to just stuff his feet in his fucking shoes. I want to just sit his butt down on the potty. Because I'm bigger than he is and stronger, and I could make him do what I need him to do in a tenth of the fucking time.

I struggle with the ability to "invite his cooperation," because I know I have the ability to control him, physically. I could hold him down. I have, before. On days when I've lost my way, after a crap night of sleep, near the end of the week, after he head-butted Buster or used a toothbrush (mine) to clean his poopy butt.

You don't get it.
You just don't get it.
You do what I say.
I'm in charge here.
I'm the biggest.
I'm the strongest.
I'm the fucking boss.
This is what I want.
This is what's normal and expected of us.
I'm going to do it now.
Understand?

I'm ashamed to say that sometimes I insist for no good reason other than to prove I am The Insister. I make him get a diaper change this instant, rather than getting on his level to explain what's happening. I try to convince myself that I'm insisting because external needs are forcing my hand; look at the time! We'll be late for school!

We could have been late to school. But I hate being late to school. Besides, I wanted to *show* him. When he got angry and kicked, I stopped him from kicking. Which is another way of saying I held his legs down. And please understand, when I say it felt good that he got upset, it isn't that I enjoyed his sadness. It's that I was glad, for a second, that I wasn't the only one who felt like shit.

Sometimes there just isn't time to get permission.

———

I went to college with a woman who dated a barely-famous man who was outed, recently, as an abuser and a rapist. She spoke up. She told her story to protect the other women he'd dated who were being slandered as false accusers.

———

When I told people I was having a boy, and then another boy, most often they'd say, "Oh, I bet you're relieved! Girls are a lot of worry." I understood what they meant. Because, raising boys, I don't have to worry about one of them coming home pregnant, right? Because since I've got a house full of d and no v, I don't have to avoid news stories about teenage girls getting gang-raped by the high school football team. Because if I'm a mother of sons, those stories don't scare me, right?

No. False. I'm just as terrified by sexual violence as any woman, as any mother of any child, boy or girl. As a mother of sons, I worry about my babies becoming victims. I also have nightmares about my boys becoming perpetrators.

If modern media coverage of sexual assault has devastatingly betrayed women, it has also done a fine job of sensationalizing the white-bred clean-cut boy-next-door rapist, chino-clad and looking like a man in size, and like a boy in his fear, as he waits for the verdict that could change his life.

(Feminist Werewolf Says: *Wow! You get a trial? You're lucky. We usually just get raped. No, but yours has evidence and a judge to make sure your sentence is fair? For you? That's great. For you. Congratulations on that.)*

Like survivors of rape and abuse, perpetrators of rape and abuse come from anywhere. On the top-three list of things I'm afraid of fucking up as a parent, "failing to teach my sons to respect other people, and particularly other women, not because women are more deserving of respect than men, but because women are more physically vulnerable than men" is like #2 on that list. Right underneath "failing to teach him to not murder."

And as I have deepened my relationship with my charming, challenging, screaming, pinching children, I have to get comfortable knowing that there is some part of me that understands the mindset of a person whose impulse to control others exceeds his limits of socialization, empathy, and self-control.

I mean, every person who does something shitty has somehow talked him or herself into it, right?

I stole my mom's diamond earrings but she left us for a week once when we were kids, and I needed to pay the rent.

I shook my daughter, but she KNOWS she shouldn't touch my work papers and there have been layoffs so I'm really stressed. I feel bad about it, but what was I supposed to do?

I listened to my friend talk about what it was like living with and loving someone who did a lot of shitty stuff to her - who shamed her, harmed her, violated her. I think, somehow he talked himself into this. I think, how is it fucking possible that he thinks this is okay? Because he *does*. In the Wicked Broadway musical version of his life, somehow, these women pulled the poison out of him. It is the human condition to believe your own bullshit when there's a payoff on the line.

I can't help but wonder if his mom ever just stuffed his fucking feet into his shoes. I wonder if she ever felt, the way I often do, that it would just be easier to *make* people do what I want them to do.

Please don't misunderstand me - good God, I would never blame a parent for an adult child's actions. I don't doubt that this man was once a child who was raised with love. I don't think, as the old joke goes, that it's all the mother's fault.

Except, you know, when I'm the mother who could be blamed. As a parent, I would never consider blaming the mom for the sins of the son. As a parent, I would never be able to not blame myself if it were my son who'd sinned. I wouldn't be able to help but remember all the times I looked at my son and thought, "JUST DO WHAT I SAY!"

Is that not the textbook shriek of a mother on the edge? Is that not the textbook defense of an abuser? Is my son watching me now? Now? Now?

Is he learning?

————

I've never been hit or raped, and I've never hit anyone in anger except my sister when she caught me wearing her Delia*s baby tee with the cherries embroidered on it.

I have never hurt my children. I cannot imagine hurting them, which is to say I have been angry enough to imagine it, and then immediately fell to my knees to reach out with hands that said "I'm sorry," even though they'd never done anything to apologize for.

I've been in my fair share of unpleasant relationships, threatening moments, scary encounters, rooms in which I was keenly aware of being outweighed, outmatched, at mercy. If my head were *Inside Out*, there'd be a character of Womanhood voiced by Fairuza

Balk who would tell me when it was time to go dark, because shit's about to get nasty. Ask a girl, any girl. She's got these stories.

We girls have babies. Some of them are boys and some are girls. Some will grow up to fuck people up, and some will not. Is it about power? Is it about parenting?

Talk about the human condition... I could find order in a bag of spilled rice, wisdom in the way those grains lay, if I wanted it bad enough - my condemnation, or my pardon. I could find the signs. I am, after all, a product of a world that makes women do things they don't want to do, and then be sorry that they got hurt in the process, and then shut the fuck up about it.

I'm trying to carve out a new road for my kids. Every day I'm aware of another time I gave up and forced. Every day I remember another time I gave up, and was forced. I think about power - bigger men, stronger voices in chorus, a nameplate on a desk. How it's made me, shushed me, hurt people I love, poisoned the thoughts of those who hurt them.

I still, God help me, yearn for it. I lust for it. I hunger, in dark places, for the ability to stop hands, change minds, freeze the large bodies of others before they make stains, before they make scars.

I say, to my son, "please, stop. Please listen to me."

New Math

Here's where you watch me try to be the bigger person here and unpack why it pisses me off so much that we're raising a generation of girls who believe that a woman has to tick a certain number of boxes that were drawn by other people without her input in order to be considered a success.

WAIT. DO I? Seriously? Do I *still* have to explain why it bothers me that we're determining the level of a woman's value by whether or not her choices conform to what the rest of the herd thinks is valuable?

Okay, after I'm done perhaps you can catch my follow-up lectures: "Squares: They Have Four Sides," and "When it Rains You Might Want an Umbrella, or You Will Get Wet." I'll call it my "Are You Fucking Kidding Me With This - A Lecture Series in Remedial Humanity."

Here we go.

Are You Fucking Kidding Me With This
Lecture 1:
(Girls + Math) - (Girls + Baking) = Fake Feminism

There's this huge trend right now in children's media - Girl astronauts! Girl scientists! Girl explorers! Girl engineers! And that is FANTASTIC. I'm not trying to Grinch on increasing female representation in STEM. It just seems like girl poets, girl caregivers, girl cupcake bakers, and girl knitters are getting a lot of flak.

Or not flak, exactly. It's not as though we punish girls who develop interests in traditionally female fields. We just don't talk about them so much. We definitely don't call them "cool." Doctor girls and scientist girls and hard rock-drummer girls and all the girls pursuing traditionally male interests, they're getting all the glory.

These are our daughters, Suzie and Annabelle. Annabelle wants to be an engineer! Isn't that AWESOME?

Oh, and Suzie writes poems.

I've been thinking a lot about this long-overdue celebration of girls (as long as they're girls who like science) and I am coming down hard.   This is fake feminism.

Even if we're praising girls for being great at math and science, we're still not praising them for being *who they are*; we're praising them for daring to be girls who pursue what we still think of as *boy* things.

We haven't evolved enough to be able to admire a girl's tenacity or creativity or curiosity, her innate character. We've just become good enough at branding ourselves and each other that we recognize the value of the unexpected combo - she wears pink AND knows how to code? Ka- CHING!

I love a girl power book or movie as much as the next person, but it seems to me that we're selling ourselves a little too cheap and easy. Make a movie about a girl who invents something and we're SOLD. Write a book about a girl who plays baseball and we will tell all our friends. I can't shake the feeling that Disney hired a crack team of social media analysts to write Frozen.

Where's the trendy new book celebrating a girl who learned how to quilt? Where's the movie about a girl who changed the world with her volunteerism? When the stories that glorify "women's work" make millions, that's when we can start being proud of ourselves.

But today, the fact that we are so proud of girls who excel in math shows how much we still value math, not how much we've come to value girls.

But what about girls (OR BOYS, for that matter) who really love "girly" things?

Oh, them? They're probably off baking somewhere, making quilts and trying to remember how to count to seven. Don't worry, they're simple folk. Probably raised by stay-at-home mothers, poor dears. Never had a chance for success...

No! False!

Quilting is precise, detailed work. You know, like surgery. Coding requires creativity, patience, and sharp problem-solving skills. You know, like parenting. Still not getting the message? Alright, here it is, math-style:

I.
GIRLS = BOYS

II.
GIRLS who like math = BOYS who like math

IIIa.
GIRLS who are hungry to learn all they can about math
or coding
or medicine
or racecar driving
=
GIRLS who are hungry to learn all they can about sewing
or drawing
or non-profit work
or parenting

IIIb.
BOYS who are hungry to learn all they can about math
or coding
or medicine
or racecar driving
=

BOYS who are hungry to learn all they can about sewing
or drawing
or non-profit work
or parenting.

    If we are going to be feminists, we have to tell our children that they can become whatever they want to be. And we have to mean it. Even if she doesn't want to be an astronaut. Even if she wants to bake wedding cakes. Even if she wants to be a secretary at a law office instead of an attorney, or a Red Bull promotional model.
    Even if she wants to be a stay-at-home mother and spend her days folding onesies and swabbing down her children's poopy bottoms (showing them, at least six times a day, that they deserve love, that they are worth messy, stinky, hard work) and helping them play inventor, truck driver, babysitter, cake-baker (showing them that the world is full of fascinating endeavors, no matter what junk they got by the luck of the chromosomal draw.)
    Even if he wants to be a stay-at-home father and spend the afternoon searching for slow-cooker recipes because Thursdays are go go go since we went back to school. Even if he never earns a penny or a promotion. When we start to value his parenting as much as we value her engineering, that's when we can start being proud of ourselves.

That's all this feminist werewolf has to say about that.

Ice Ice Babies

I stand alone at a crossroads. The stakes have never been higher. My son's futures - and maybe even the future of society at large - are at stake.

In my house, consent is nonnegotiable. My top priority as a parent is to raise sons who respect themselves and ALL others. In our home, when someone says "STOP," I want the response to be instinctive, drilled in, incontrovertible. Stop. Not giggling. Not joking. Not "I know he didn't mean that." Just stop.

And yet.

And yet.

This morning I discovered that this conversation *could* be part of my daily life:

Buster (2):   STOP!
Chicken (4):   Collaborate and listen!

Holy. Fucking. Shit.

With three little words, my world just blew wide open. I have to choose. Do I raise nice, nice babies... or ice, ice babies?

Do I raise men who hold women in high regard, or men whose high top and fade is the stuff of 90's legend?

Are my grown-up sons going to be like, "If there's a problem, yo I'll solve it," or "If there's a problem, yo I am happy to help if you ask, but I believe that you are just as capable of solving it as I am, because girl, I'm not a plumber either."

Do I want my sons to have a vibe that says, "Will I ever stop? Yes, immediately, when you look uncomfortable or say no," or "Will I ever stop? Yo, you don't know."

Do I want Chicken to be like, "Deadly, when I play a dope melody," or "Rapey, when I dope your appletini."

Will Buster be like, "Girlies on standby, I'm waving just to say hi... and tell you to smile because society has programmed me to think I'm entitled to your attention," OR will he be like "Flying to Duluth on standby, I'm waving just to say hi... because we went to high school together and I can't believe I'm running into you at the airport! So what have you been up to?"

(Runner-up for that last one: "Flying to Duluth on standby, waving just to say hi... excuse me, you dropped your keys, here they are, have a nice day and I won't try to hug you or smell your hair.")

Like, at my son's rehearsal dinner do I want his future wife to stand up and tell the story of how they met and be like, "Someone grabbed ahold of me tightly," or "Someone asked if he could grab ahold of me tightly, and I thought about it and said, 'No, I'm not comfortable with that yet,' and he responded, 'Okay, I'm fine with that. Let's get a coffee and you can tell me more about your favorite books,' and I said, 'That sounds nice.'"

You tell me, dear reader. You tell me.

The Day Before

I went on vacation, and it was glorious. I peed when I had to pee. I went to the gym. I got a massage, and I took a nap, and then I went to dinner and a movie with my girls.

But at what cost, you ask? As I prepared to leave my family for the weekend, I realized, again, that everything is unfair and my job is sometimes horse shit.

The day before I went on vacation, I stocked the fridge, bought a couple of little new toys for the boys that they could not open until the weekend, as an act of mercy for my husband.

I also did seven loads of laundry, cleaned out the fridge, wrote out our emergency contact information, filled out the enrollment paperwork for the kids' new school that is due next week, printed the forms for Chicken's summer camp next week, and made copies of the boys' health insurance cards.

I also packed a weekend backpack with clothes, diapers, snacks, water bottles, a first aid kit, some emergency cash, the library card, sunscreen, and another emergency contact sheet.

Then I had a glass of wine. I was, after all, almost on vacay! All I had to do at that point was pack, clean the bathroom, and write out the stuff for the sitter.

At 8:30 I started the letter to the babysitter, a wonderful person who has known our kids since Buster was born. She knows them, knows our basic routine, and this isn't the first time she's spent a long chunk of time caring for them.

In other words, she knows what's up. So I thought writing the letter would take no more than 10 minutes - jot down a quick schedule, hit the highlights (binkies in the top drawer, diapers in the bottom drawer, lock them in if you don't want to chase them down the street or fish them out of the river. You know, basic.)

But as I typed I started to think of helpful tips to add here and there. I typed "go to library," and realized that without some inside information, a pleasant outing to a chapel of knowledge could easily turn into a cautionary after-school special: "No Exit: I'll Never Let Go: Paper Screams: The Chicken and Buster Story." So I added:

"It's easiest to get them to leave the library if you talk about leaving before you arrive. Before you even walk into the library, explain exactly what will happen when you say it's time to go, and then the transition is usually a lot easier."

And that got me thinking. How much of what I do as a parent is indescribably complicated? How much of our work is unspoken, yet exhausting?

It's like we never stopped being pregnant. When I grew a baby inside my body, where the work happened in a place where people couldn't see my effort, where I rarely broke a sweat, where nobody marveled at my strength, because the effort occurred on a cellular level, and where in fact people were often confused as to why I was so tired.

"I'm exhausted," I said at work.

"Um, you're sitting on a chair," a coworker quipped. Hilariously.

"AND I AM BUILDING A HUMAN. FROM SCRATCH," I replied.

Because I was pregnant, she backed away slowly and nodded and fawned over me and brought me her leftovers from the taco stand.

I accepted her offerings and blessed her with my mercy. The tacos helped. But I did not forget. And now that I'm a parent of children who live outside my body and are sometimes annoying, I am no longer the recipient of the "Blessed Mother Mary" treatment.

At best, non-parent strangers treat me like a "good mom" which means my unflagging and cheerful work will be both constant and unremarkable; at worst, they treat me like I'm a "hot mess" and my kids are obviously doomed. If I express feelings of exhaustion, those feelings are met with skepticism and silence.

"I'm exhausted," I might say.

"But you are sitting on a bench at the park," they might think. "And also where is that smoke coming from?"

It's coming from my ears, nostrils, and throat, because every time I have to justify that my work does, in fact, exist, and not only does it exist, but it is omnipresent and eternal, the only thing that can get me through that conversation is a fiery ball of righteous indignation.

Who run the world? Women. Moms. Women run the *world*.

I seriously would not be surprised to learn that gravity is just something that a grandma in Louisville has been handling, quietly, just in the back of her mind, while she makes biscuits for 400 people for the church jamboree.

I have decided there is only one solution for the widespread cultural blindness to the constant and necessary and unacknowledged work that moms do.

Dear Pixar,

Please make an animated short film about everything that happens inside a mother's mind while she is sitting on a bench at the park. Do good. You don't want to cross us.

Love,

The World-Runners

Girls

Girls have a reputation
for talking too much
for caring about girl stuff
like dolphins
and split ends,

for manipulation
for resentment
for passive aggression
for feelings. Lord,
bleeding curtains of stormy feelings.

Girls have a reputation for respecting women
who are not beautiful
and suspecting women
who are.

Girls get a raw deal,
I think.

Just now.
That.

Girls say
I think
rather than
This is true.

Maybe because
we think
we have to
in order to avoid being
abrasive.

Maybe because
we think
it's easier for people to smile at opinions than facts.
And it's nice to make someone smile!

Girls are aware
early on
there is danger in being outweighed
there is a price for being outspoken
there is a time when it's ok to be outsmarted.

My 7th grade math teacher
divided us
into boys versus girls
for an algebra relay race.
On the blackboard,
he wrote "Boys" on one side,
and on the other side,
"The Weaker Sex."

That school cost

significantly more than the state university
per year.
He was joking
I think
and perhaps inviting a person
to prove him wrong.

But all the boys laughed
and jumped out of toppling chairs
to high-five each other
and the girls exchanged open-mouthed silences,
sitting frozen as a colony of shocked squirrels.

Hot-cheeked, I picked up my chair
and carried it to the door.
I placed my chair just over the threshold and sat
with my back to the class.
The teacher told me to come back inside.
I sat still.
I wasn't very good at math anyway.

Girls have a very specific set of skills.
Generally speaking,
most girls I know have a
dependable
crowd-pleasing
side dish they can bring to a dinner party,
a
sweet
soft
sinful
cookie recipe in case of afternoon company,
and a
virtuous
nourishing
salad in case there's a barbeque.

Most girls I know have an unconscious defense
mechanism
when faced with a threat
or a douchebag.
Most girls I know make themselves smaller
and less
like the first Billy Goat Gruff:
"who, me? I'm just a little nothing. You don't want me,
Mr. Troll."

Most girls I know have a friend who starves.
Most girls I know have a friend whose boyfriend is
cheating.
Most girls I know have a friend who has been hit.
Most girls I know have a friend who has been raped.
Most girls I know would talk for hours about these things
in a room of women.
But not if men were around.
We wouldn't want to make anyone uncomfortable.

Girls have to be careful
when they walk places
or answer the door
and also when they compose their emails.

My boss once told me that I could be abrasive.
He wasn't wrong,
I guess.
I said, "Can you give me an example
of a time that my
abrasiveness
has impacted my work?"
and he said,
"I can't think of anything right now."
I said, "I'll follow up with you on this.

I would hate to think that I'm unintentionally
offending
anyone."
He said, "Actually, right now is an example."

Girls don't get hungry
until they're starving.

It's awesome to watch a thin girl eat a whole pizza.
It's annoying to watch a thin girl eating a single carrot
stick.
It's embarrassing to watch a big girl eat a whole pizza.
It's sad to watch a big girl eat a single carrot stick.

Girls eat vengefully.
Have you noticed this?
Girls eat salads for revenge on their shorts.
Girls eat cheeseburgers for revenge on their judgmental
great-aunts.

I once gagged while eating a slab of carrot cake that I did
not want
because an elderly relative had patted my leg with her dry
hand
and reminded me that I'd soon need to fit into my
wedding dress.
Boy,
I showed her.

Girls feel like old news
I think.
Or at least I do.
Still? Still, we're talking about
girls
as if we don't know them?
As if the hundreds of years of dialogue

about women
just here,
just in this country,
were on some other station
and you're just now tuning in
but we've been talking about it
for
ever
and I'm tired of talking about girls.

I'm tired of waiting outside an office
where I know someone will look at me
with an incredulous face
and say
but you can vote
and work in any job
and nobody is going to try to kill you for your family's
honor
or anything like that.
For God's sake,
Miss,
what more do you want?
We're not the thought police.
We can't legislate what's in people's heads.

Just what's in their wombs, then?
Just the part that belongs only to girls?

We're not hungry until we're starving.
We don't want to make anyone uncomfortable.
We're not sure how not to be abrasive.

Girls have a reputation
for holding a grudge
for drinking Chardonnay
for feelings

bleeding curtains of stormy feelings

for snapping at their children
for sleeping their way up
for crying
for talking too much
about stupid shit
like dolphins and split ends
and babies.

Actually,
right now is an example.

My son told me yesterday
that if he were a worm
and could pick which to be
he'd rather be a girl
when he's alone
but a boy the other times.
I asked him why, and he said
"Girls are really strong
but they always wait.
I'd like to be strong
like a girl.
But it seems really hard
to be a girl."

I've seen the girls in his class
and he's right.
They are strong.
They're organized, too.
They have plans
and execute them
as a team.

And when the snacks come out,

Katie Anthony

they sit, exchanging silent glances
while the boys topple their chairs.

I didn't realize
it took only three years to learn,
for girls.

We Are in Pain

There is pain in the daily experience of being female.

There is pain in being a sexual object before you are sexually empowered. Think of baby turtles in the vast ocean - soft, tasty morsels without the hard shells they'll need to survive. There's pain in being catcalled as a child, in being shunned by other girls for growing breasts before they do, in smiling at disgusting jokes because the other option is to start a fight with someone bigger and louder than you are. There is pain in knowing your relative size, and weakness.

You know the conventional wisdom that tells you, knowingly, that "the first time hurts a little"? Translation: there is pain in sex. There is pain in being the one who MUST go to Planned Parenthood for birth control or the morning-after pill (whereas your partner can go to Planned Parenthood or Taco Bell, either's good, because whether he puts a penis, Plan B, or a Gordita Baja in his body, Josh is not going to find himself ticking off days in his calendar in 3 weeks, wondering if he will still be able to graduate college.)

There is pain in trying to be seen as an equal. There is pain in not being called on in class. There is pain in knowing that you have to try. There's pain in going to a church where only men stand as elders, in looking around at all the women in the pews. There's pain in speaking to men and seeing yourself ignored. There is pain when someone meets my husband and me and shakes his hand but not mine.

I can only speak to my experience of being a girl and a woman, but I can tell you that I was made to feel most valuable when I was pleasing, easy, sparkling and inconsequential.

What the world most values about me is at odds with what I most value about myself, and there is deep pain in that. Because it means that either the world and the people I love in the world are wrong (which is scary and lonely) or I am wrong (which is the definition of shame.)

Consider how much pain there is, even in this woman's first-world life. A few sketchy hookups and shitty microaggressions here and there do not make me Malala.

And then consider the woman you are, the women you love, the woman you're raising. She hurts too. These things and others like them hurt her. We are in pain.

NEXT-LEVEL RAGE STROKE:

HARVEY FUCKING WEINSTEIN

OK SO QUICK RECAP.

Harvey Weinstein sexually assaults women. I use that verb tense consciously - it is a present tense action, a choice that he makes over and over again and has become synonymous with his character. Brad Pitt eats onscreen a lot. Harvey Weinstein sexually assaults women.

If you are a woman (or a particularly foxy ficas) and have been in a room with Harvey Weinstein at any point over the last 20 years, then it's likely that you have been pressured, pushed, manipulated, intimidated, literally chased, grabbed, groped, and bullied into compromising your safety and self-respect. Make no mistake, this man is a violent predator.

When the news broke, I remember thinking something along the lines of, "Yep. What a prick. Mm hmm."

As I scrolled down the list of known assaults, I began to get an image of Harvey Weinstein as a rhinoceros that had guzzled a crate of Viagra, and then gone charging through the world with a furious scaly rhino dong, grabbing women, demanding massages, ready to pop off into any wet hole or leafy cavity that happened to cross his path.

We've all met one of those bros. Am I right, ladies?

I'm not even going to touch Harvey Weinstein's actual statement because that's been so thoroughly eviscerated that I feel like we're all good there. I feel like his worthless garbage apology, like "meh meh meh I grew up in the 60's" (oh you mean like Mr. Rogers you bag of angry dicks) has been beaten with cudgels, set aflame, and then stomped into a fine ashy silt by a million screaming women and, like, they were very thorough. There's nothing more for me to do there.

What I do want to talk about is how dudes are talking about this guy. The famous people comments and statements, plus just the general man approach on "the Harvey Weinstein scandal."

Everyone's so fucking shocked that Harvey Weinstein is a monster. There must be "two Harvey Weinsteins" according to Jeffrey Katzenberg! Holy shit, J Katz blew the lid off this case. TWO HARVEY WEINSTEINS! He's a MASTER OF ILLLUSION!

It couldn't possibly be the case that a wealthy white dude studio head has selective awareness of another wealthy white dude studio head's shitty rape habit, because if he doesn't look directly into the faces of the women who have been shittily raped by the second wealthy white dude studio head, everyone can keep making lots and lots of money.

No no, you're good, Jeff. You figured out a way to make sure you can't possibly be blamed for this. Good job. Now all you have to do is leak your email denouncing Harvey fucking Weinstein to the Hollywood Reporter, leak that you anonymously donated some money to some rape charity somewhere, maybe the Lady Gaga one from the Oscars a couple years ago, and you're golden.

Everyone's so certain that this kind of behavior is unacceptable! Appalling! Nauseating! I wouldn't be surprised to hear that Thesaurus.com went dark in the hours after the Weinstein story broke, when all the publicists rushed to their laptops to find other words that mean "ew."

Everyone has DAUGHTERS! And SISTERS! And MOMS! And WIVES! Is *that* what it takes for a man to find sexual assault scary and disgusting? Having a daughter/sister/mom/wife? Sweet Lord, I would hate to see what those fucking Bradys were up to before they met that lovely lady we've heard so much about.

All of these men are out there beating their chests at each other, like, BRO, you hate rape? I hate rape too! WE ARE GOOD MEN.

They're expounding at the top of their lungs on the profound levels of shock and disgust and outrage, and fawning over the heroes who have come forward at great personal cost and vowing that they will speak up next time!

I swear to God, if one more white-toothed millionaire tells me that he will never let this happen on HIS watch, I am going to start punching wieners.

Gentlemen. Gather.

I hear you. You are shocked. You have daughters. You wish to express your outrage and solidarity with women. You wish to let us know that you would protect us from harm. You think Harvey Weinstein is a monster. You proclaim that we must ALL do better for our women.

None of this is "incorrect." These are all "right" answers. And I know you genuinely feel upset and angry and staggered at the scope of the crime. But I'm going to bring you into the inner circle right now, guys:

I DON'T REALLY BELIEVE YOU. NONE OF US DO. We can't afford to.

I know and like *hundreds* of nice guys, and I trust 3 men on this entire fucking Earth.

Gentlemen, no matter how nice you are, how many lady friends you have, how happily married, how many daughters you have sired, and how many chick flicks you've watched and then said, "Hey, that was actually pretty good," 99.9% of the women in your life are reserving about 10% of their opinion of you. We are waiting.

We are waiting for you to have too many drinks one night. We are waiting for you to compliment our new jeans in front of the boss at work. We're waiting for you to interrupt us and explain our experience back to us - "You weren't actually catcalled, he just really liked your shirt." We aren't waiting because it's fun, or we're crazy. But because it happens. all. the. fucking. time. We have to hang back a bit and wait for your inner dirtbag to show himself because experience has shown us that he always fucking does.

So I believe that you *mean* everything you're saying today. I believe you want to protect women from Harvey Weinstein. I believe you genuinely want a safer world for girls.

I just don't believe you can be part of that safer world. Not yet. Not while you're still SHOCKED that Harvey fucking Weinstein is a piece of shitty, shitty shit.

Because you're *shocked*?

Really? Really. REALLY? Pay a-fucking-ttention, CHAD.

When you chew up fifteen minutes of my day expressing your total galloping dumbfounded astonishment that the guy that every woman in Hollywood knew was a predator turned out to be a fucking predator, that tells me three things: 1) You don't talk to very many women about what it's like to be a woman, and 2) You don't listen to me, ever, and 3) you don't believe women when they tell you that something feels creepy, off, or weird about Harvey.

I guarantee you *this* conversation happened about 40,000 times over the last 20 years:

> Female Actress: Hey, Harvey just asked me to meet in his hotel room tonight about the script.
> Male Actor: Oh really?
> FA: Yeah, did he ask you too?
> MA: No... but I'm sure it's fine.
> FA: I don't know, it feels a little weird.
> MA: Listen, it's Harvey Weinstein. It's fine.
> FA: I guess, but, you know, you hear things.
> MA: People love to talk about powerful guys. Everyone wants to take him down.
> FA: Yeah, that's true.
> MA: You're probably just nervous. This could be a great opportunity for you.
> FA: You're right.

Don't be fucking *shocked*, Chad. Your shock might be your attempt to empathize with me. You might be trying to imagine how we women feel. The next time you hear some guy honking or whistling or hollering at us on the street, look at our faces, Chad. All the lady faces. Do we look shocked to you.

Fuck no, we don't look shocked. We look fucking tired. We look like this smells like the same shit stew that we have to stomach day in and day out, and you just walked into the room and you're like doing the pre-vomit saliva pool, gagging at the stench. I know. I live here, dude.

You say you're shocked to show me you're on my team. But your shock shows me you aren't on my team. Your shock asks me to comfort or reassure you. Your shock tells me that my life is something you don't actually want to know about.

If you were on my team you would be listening to me explain why I'm not fucking shocked. You would listen to me tell you that everything Harvey Weinstein did is both outrageously despicable, and totally fucking standard.

Oh, and you're calling for men to *condemn this behavior when they see it*? OK, first of all, that's a pretty low bar to clear. OBVIOUSLY, in the wake of a sensational firing of a prominent and powerful man for sexual assault, what sane person is going to come out in favor of the behavior of repeatedly bullying and manipulating women into unwilling sexual...

... OKAY, BESIDES THE PRESIDENT OF THE UNITED STATES. We all knew that one. That was a gimme.

Condemn this behavior when they see it? Bitch, please. You won't see it. Not because Harvey Weinstein was like a master of deception. But because he is rich and was powerful and you wanted something from him, and the thing you wanted from him mattered way more than whether he literally chased a young girl around the room and forced her to touch his penis and then she left Hollywood and gave up on her lifelong dream of acting because the experience was so humiliating and traumatic.

You think he's a *monster*! I bet you sincerely do. I bet you really think that he's an awful violent beast. Here's the problem. When you call him a monster, you are creating distance between you and Harvey Weinstein.

It gives you a sense of absolution that you have not earned. Like, "Well I'VE never lunged at a young woman and tried to stuff my hand up her skirt and into her vagina while she screamed and tried to run away. I'm obviously a feminist." Or, "I've never refused to work with someone because she refused to suck my dick. I am a friend to the ladies." Or, "I think rape is gross. Clearly, I've never hurt a woman." False, Chad. False. False forever. False all over your face.

You need to take a deep breath and a hard look at your life, and you need to look for all of the places where you are *exactly* like Harvey fucking Weinstein. Because those places are there. Yes, in you, Matt Damon.

Have you ever felt entitled to a woman's time or energy?

Have you ever talked over a woman coworker or excluded her from a project because it would be easier socially without her?

Have you ever been annoyed when a woman caused a problem with a complaint against a co-worker?

Have you ever interrupted a woman?

Have you ever felt angry at her when she was direct with you?

Have you ever called your ex crazy?

Have you ever looked the other way when someone was being an asshole to a woman?

Just because you aren't this particular brand of dirtbag doesn't make you Maya fucking Angelou, Chad. You have misogyny in you. Everyone does. Every man in America can do better at respecting women, and I include in that statement literally every man in America. Did I fucking stutter?

If you want to be a friend to the ladies, stop being shocked. I seriously cannot get over everyone's SHOCK. Every time you're STILL FUCKING SHOCKED, it insults me.

Unless... did you just emerge from a time capsule like Brendan Fraser in Blast from the Past? Are we about to have a fucking malted and look at your mint-condition baseball cards together and fall in love in totally predictable beats? Have you seriously never heard of a public figure abusing women? Are you also flabbergasted at the sight of a goddamned magic keyfob that unlocks all the car doors at the same time?

You can only be shocked once, guys. After that you're choosing to stick your head in the sand. After that, you are making the conscious choice to continue to default to believing men instead of listening to women when they tell you something's up. Start listening to us. Believe us.

If you want to be a friend to the ladies, don't tell me what you would have done if you'd been there. Don't draw me like a fucking Super Bro comic book about how AWESOME you are at being AWESOME. Stop asking me to thank you for hypothetically saving me from something that hasn't happened to me yet. Stop picturing my devastating violation so that you can check out how swoll you look in your fantasy reel. It is fucked up. Stop it.

If you want to be a friend to the ladies, do not vow to fight anyone who tries to rape a woman in fucking front of you. That will probably never happen to you. What could easily happen to you, and definitely does, all the time, is you shit on your female coworker, or your girlfriend/wife, or a woman in line at Starbucks. Vow to learn about common ways that "nice guys" unknowingly fuck up women's days, and start to know when you do them, and then stop doing them. Not as fun as punching a dude and getting applause, I know. But it's actually better for EVERYONE. Swear to god it is.

If you want to be a friend to the ladies, Jeffrey Katzenberg, after you condemn Harvey Weinstein's admitted bad behavior and establish that THERE HAVE ALWAYS BEEN TWO HARVEY WEINSTEINS, HE'S SERIOUSLY SO METHOD, NOBODY KNEW EXCEPT EVERY WOMAN IN HOLLYWOOD AND A SHITLOAD OF LAWYERS AND THE WRITERS OF 30 ROCK, do not, I repeat though clenched teeth, DO NOT OFFER TO HELP HIM SPIN THE FUCKING SITUATION:

As someone who has been a friend of yours for 30 years, I'm available to give you advice on how to at least try to make amends, if possible address those that you've wronged, and just possibly find a path to heal and redeem yourself. Having watched your reactions, seen the actions you have taken and read your statement, I will tell you, in my opinion, you have gone about this all wrong and you are continuing to make a horrible set of circumstances even worse.

That's a piping hot gallon of hell no, JK. How about, instead:

As someone who has been a friend of yours for 30 years, I am going to offer to hire every woman that you have ever hurt, in whatever capacity she would like. I will pull every string I have and make sure that every door is open to every single woman, and I will work tirelessly to ensure that that shackles you placed on these women's careers will be removed, so help me God. I will tell you, in my opinion, that when I say that men need to step up and stand with these women, it means stepping the fuck up and standing with these fucking women, and

that is the ONLY fucking thing I can do to keep from
making a horrible set of circumstances even worse.

HOW ABOUT THAT JEFFY. HOW ABOUT
WE STOP TRYING TO HELP THE VIOLENT
SOCIOPATHIC CRIMINAL, JEFF.

And it saddens me to report that Katzenberg isn't
the only Jeff who needs to take a long fucking walk in
the woods. Jeff Bridges, the dude, one of my all-time
faves, reportedly said, in a very Dude way, "He's facing
his demons now. I hope he leans into those demons and
comes out the other side a richer person. I hope the best
for him."

I have been watching a clip of Jeff Bridges,
getting a full mug of hot coffee to the forehead for the
last 72 hours. WHAT THE FUCK, THE DUDE. That is
something you say about a guy with a heroin addiction,
not something you say about the John Wayne Gacy of
sexual assault. SERIOUSLY THE DUDE. YOU WERE
MORE ANGRY ABOUT THE FUCKING CREDENCE
TAPES than you are about Harvey fucking Weinstein's
gross, and I mean that both ways, GROSS violations of
unknown scores of women.

If it seems like I'm yelling at you, it's because I'M
YELLING AT YOU, READER.

I'M TIRED OF BEING FURIOUS ABOUT
ANGRY POWERFUL MEN.

I'M READY TO NOT HAVE TO TEACH
ANYONE HOW TO BELIEVE WOMAN VOICES.
ALL I WANT TO DO IS WRITE FUNNY JOKES
ABOUT POTTY TRAINING OKAY??? BUT THE
WORLD WE LIVE IN FUCKING HATES ME AND
WANTS TO MAKE SURE I KNOW THAT MY
VOICE IS SHRILL AND IRRITATING AND LYING
AND UNTRUSTWORTHY AND STUPID AND
EMOTIONAL AND INCAPABLE OF KNOWING

WHAT ACTUALLY HAPPENED TO ME SO WE
BETTER ASK THE GUY TO GET THE SCOOP.
THIS IS BULLSHIT. HARVEY FUCKING
WEINSTEIN IS BULLSHIT AND OUR SHOCK IS
BULLSHIT AND YOUR HERO FANTASY IS
BULLSHIT AND ALL OF OUR HOPES AND
DREAMS AND PRAYERS FOR A BETTER
TOMORROW ARE BULLSHIT.
Why are waiting until next time to speak up and
do right? We have a time right here. It's now. Let's go.
So. To recap. Again.

<u>Your natural, instinctive response when you hear about
Harvey fucking Weinstein:</u>

1. He's a monster (not like me)

2. I would have stopped it (because I'm a good guy)

3. I have daughters (so now this isn't okay anymore)

4. We need to start building a better world and calling
this out when we see it (although we don't have to see it
if it's like really uncomfortable to see it).

5. I AM SHOCKED!

<u>What we need your response to be when you hear about
Harvey fucking Weinstein:</u>

1. He's manipulated his position of power to put women
in positions of vulnerability where they couldn't choose
not to engage with him sexually without risking their
careers or reputations. I need to work harder to become
aware of my position of power, as a man, to make sure
that I am not putting women in positions of vulnerability.

2. What can I do to support women who have suffered sexual assault? This conversation isn't about how brave and strong I am, it's about the challenges that women continue to face just existing in the world.

3. Sexual assault is a violent crime that is offensive to me as a human being, not because I am related to a person who is female.

4. I am going to work on my own awareness of how I benefit from systems that keep Harvey fucking Weinstein on top for 20 years while he rapes and assaults women. I'm going to work on dismantling those systems. It's uncomfortable to see it, but I have to see it.

5. I listen to women. I believe them. I am not shocked.

OK I'm done now.

I need a drink.

ABOUT THE AUTHOR

Katie Anthony lives with her two sons
and one husband
and zero pets
in Washington state.

You can find her writing at

www.KatyKatiKate.com

Made in the USA
Middletown, DE
09 October 2018